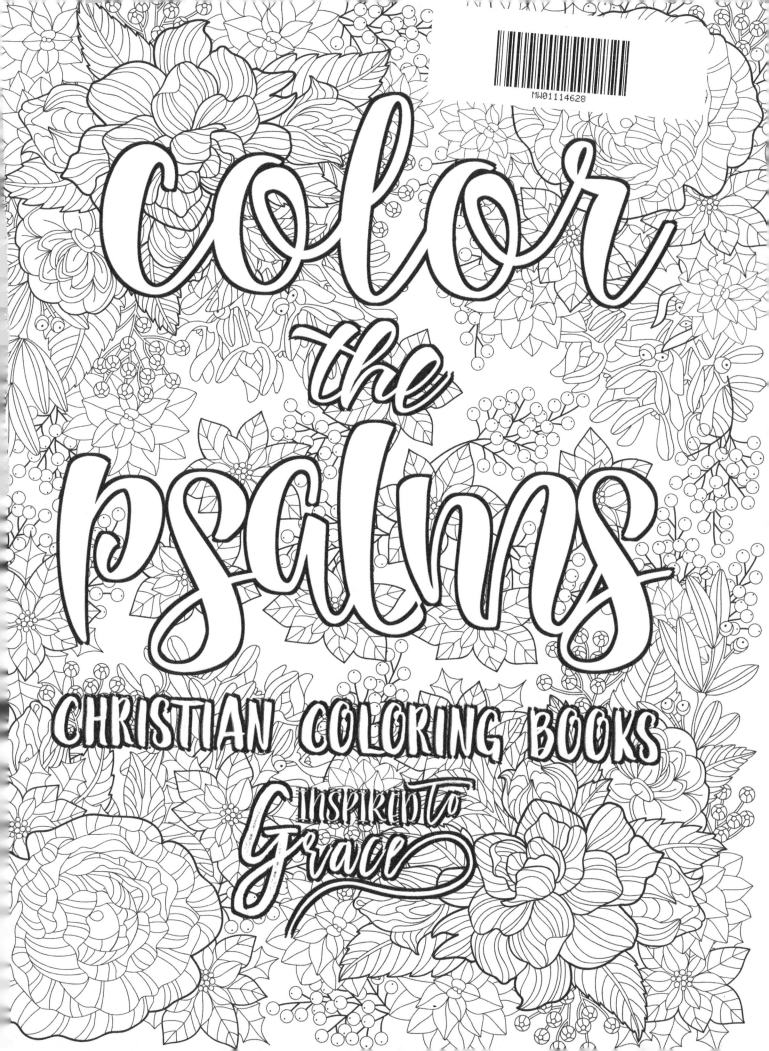

Color the Psalms

Christian Coloring Books

Inspired to Grace

Want free goodies?
Email us at freebies@inspiredtograce.com

 @inspiredtograce

 Inspired To Grace

Shop our other books at
www.inspiredtograce.com

Wholesale distribution through Ingram Content Group
www.ingramcontent.com/publishers/distribution/wholesale

For questions and customer service, email us at
support@inspiredtograce.com

Free PDF
Download of this book

www.inspiredtograce.com/ctbpsalms

YOUR DOWNLOAD CODE: CTB9337

@inspiredtograce

Inspired to Grace

The Lord is my shepherd, I shall not want. He makes me lie down in green pastures; he leads me beside still waters; he restores my soul. He leads me in right paths for his name's sake.

Psalm 23:1-3 (NRSV)

Create in me a clean heart,
O God; and renew a right spirit
within me.

Psalm 51:10 (KJV)

Have mercy on me, O God, because
of your unfailing love. Because of your
great compassion, blot out the stain
of my sins.

— Psalm 51:1 (NLT)

HAVE MERCY ON ME
O GOD
BECAUSE
OF YOUR
unfailing
LOVE
PSALM 51:1

I love you, Lord, my strength. The Lord is my rock, my fortress, and my deliverer, my God, my mountain where I seek refuge, my shield and the horn of my salvation, my stronghold. I called to the Lord, who is worthy of praise, and I was saved from my enemies.

Psalm 18:1-3 (HCSB)

Trust in the Lord and do what is good;
dwell in the land and live securely. Take
delight in the Lord, and he will give you
your heart's desires.

Psalm 37:3-4 (HCSB)

TAKE DELIGHT IN THE

Lord

PSALM 37:4

Lord, you have searched me and known me. You know when I sit down and when I stand up; you understand my thoughts from far away. You observe my travels and my rest; you are aware of all my ways. Before a word is on my tongue, you know all about it, Lord.

Psalm 139:1-4 (HCSB)

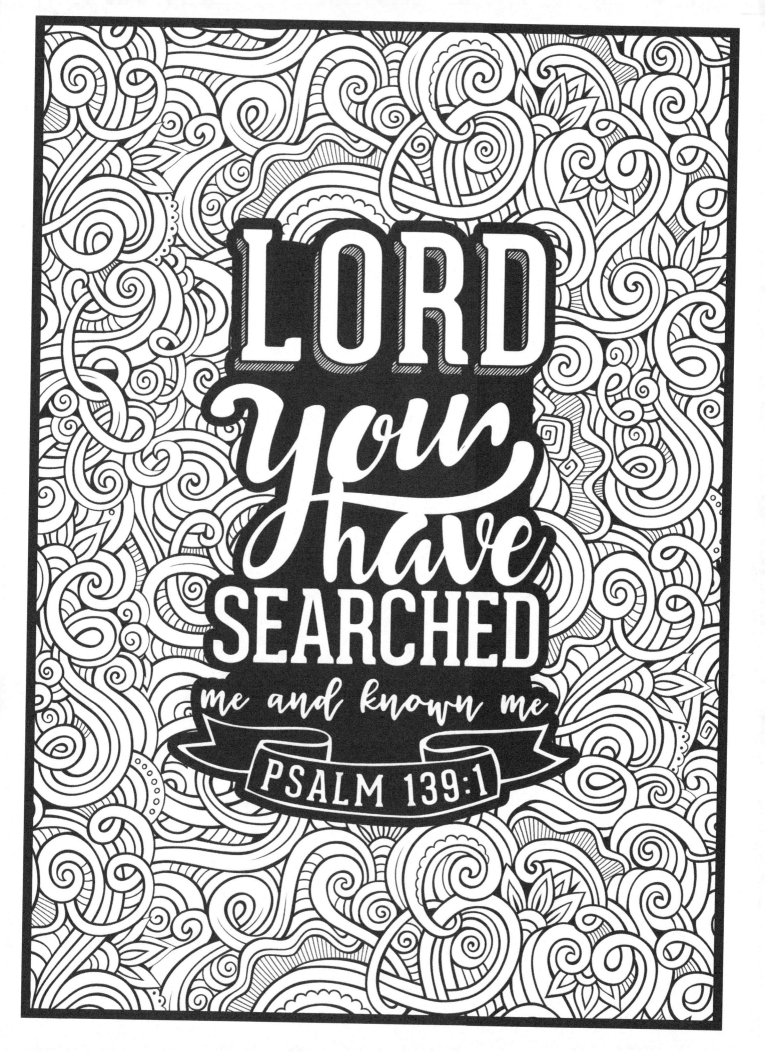

Bless the Lord,
O my soul, and all that is within me,
bless his holy name.

Psalm 103:1 (NRSV)

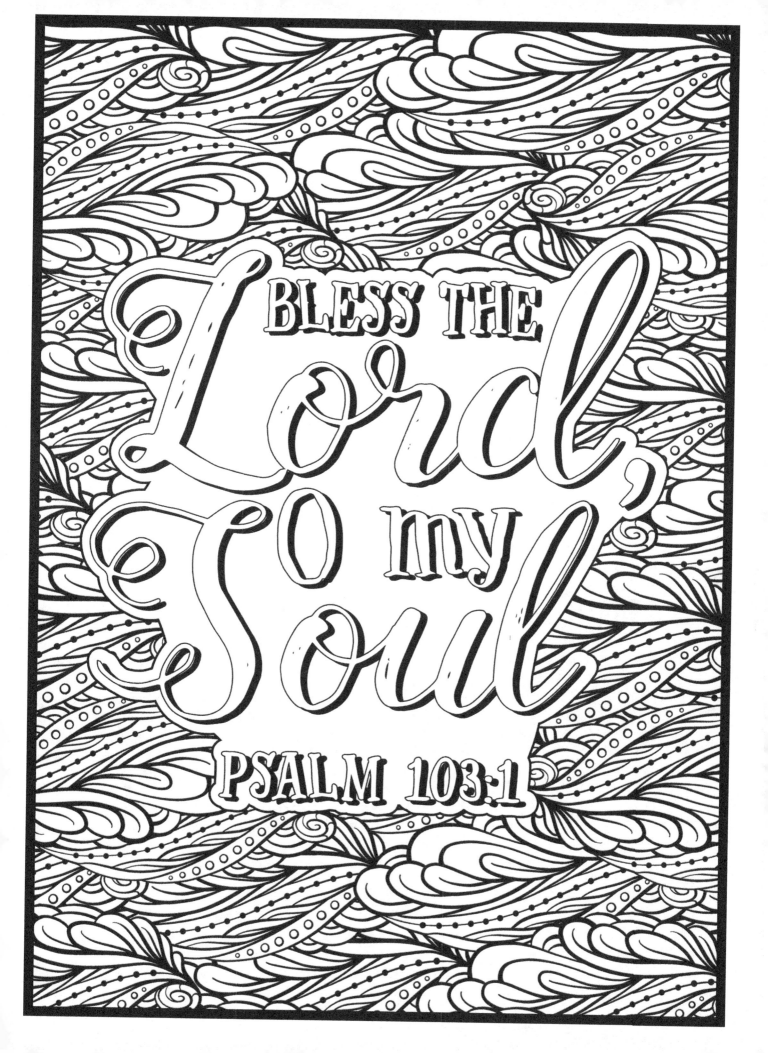

Better is one day in your courts than
a thousand elsewhere; I would rather
be a doorkeeper in the house of my God
than dwell in the tents of the wicked.
For the Lord God is a sun and shield;
the Lord bestows favor and honor; no
good thing does he withhold from those
whose walk is blameless.

Psalm 84:10-11 (NIV)

I would rather be a
DOORKEEPER
IN THE HOUSE OF MY
God
THAN DWELL IN THE
TENTS OF THE
WICKED
Psalm 84:10

You will show me the path to life,
abounding joy in your presence,
the delights at your right hand forever.

Psalm 16:11 (NABRE)

Children are a gift from the Lord;
they are a reward from him. Children
born to a young man are like arrows in
a warrior's hands. How joyful is the man
whose quiver is full of them! He will
not be put to shame when he confronts
his accusers at the city gates.

Psalm 127:3-5 (NLT)

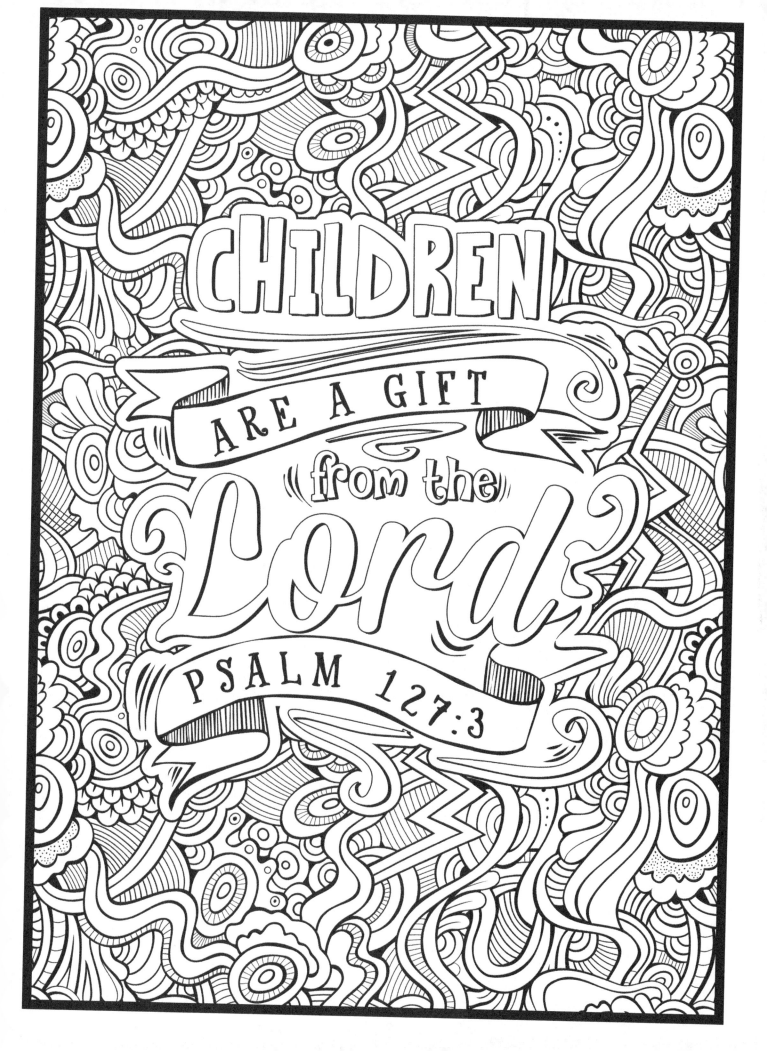

The wicked are not so, but are like chaff that the wind drives away. Therefore the wicked will not stand in the judgment, nor sinners in the congregation of the righteous; for the Lord watches over the way of the righteous, but the way of the wicked will perish.

Psalm 1:4-6 (NRSV)

The Lord is good and upright; therefore he shows sinners the way. He leads the humble in what is right and teaches them his way.

Psalm 25:8-9 (HCSB)

He leads the HUMBLE in what is right and TEACHES them his Way

PSALM 25:9

O Lord, our Lord, how awesome is your name through all the earth! I will sing of your majesty above the heavens with the mouths of babes and infants. You have established a bulwark against your foes, to silence enemy and avenger.

Psalm 8:2-3 (NABRE)

Cast your burden on the Lord,
and he shall sustain you; he shall never
permit the righteous to be moved.

Psalm 55:22 (NKJV)

I will praise you,
O Lord, with my whole heart;
I will tell of all your marvelous works.
I will be glad and rejoice in you; I will
sing praise to your name, O Most High.

Psalm 9:1-2 (NKJV)

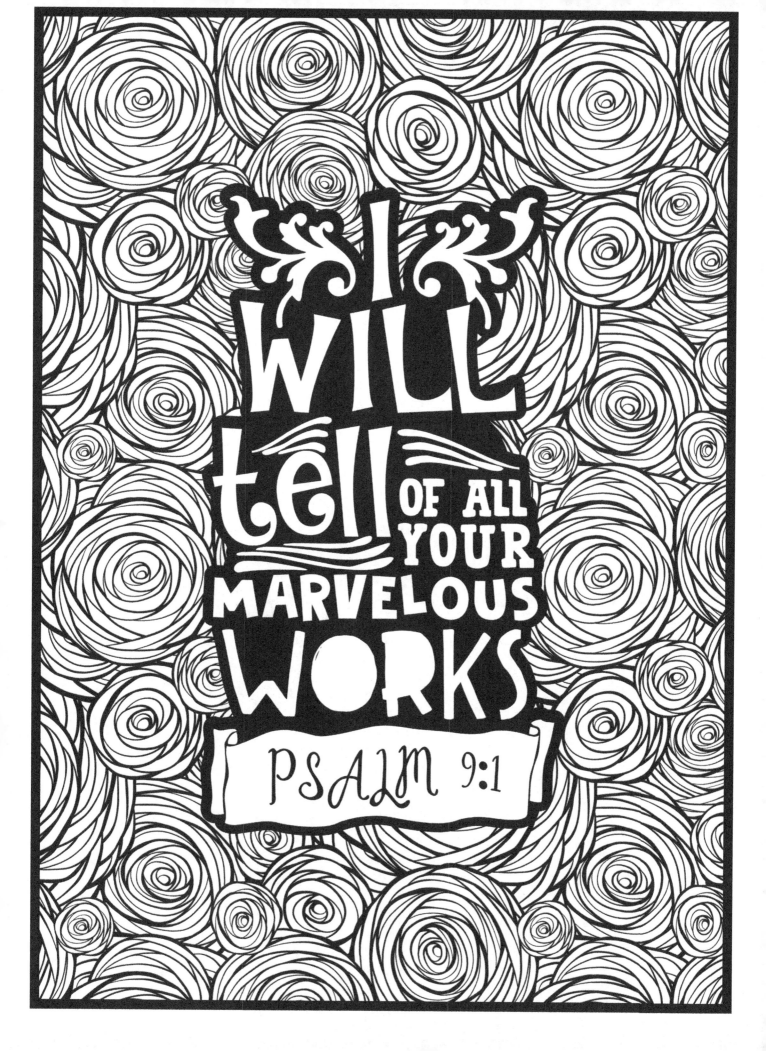

I treasure your word in my heart,
so that I may not sin against you.

Psalm 119:11 (NRSV)

I will thank the Lord in accordance
with his justice; I will sing the name
of the Lord Most High.

Psalm 7:18 (NABRE)

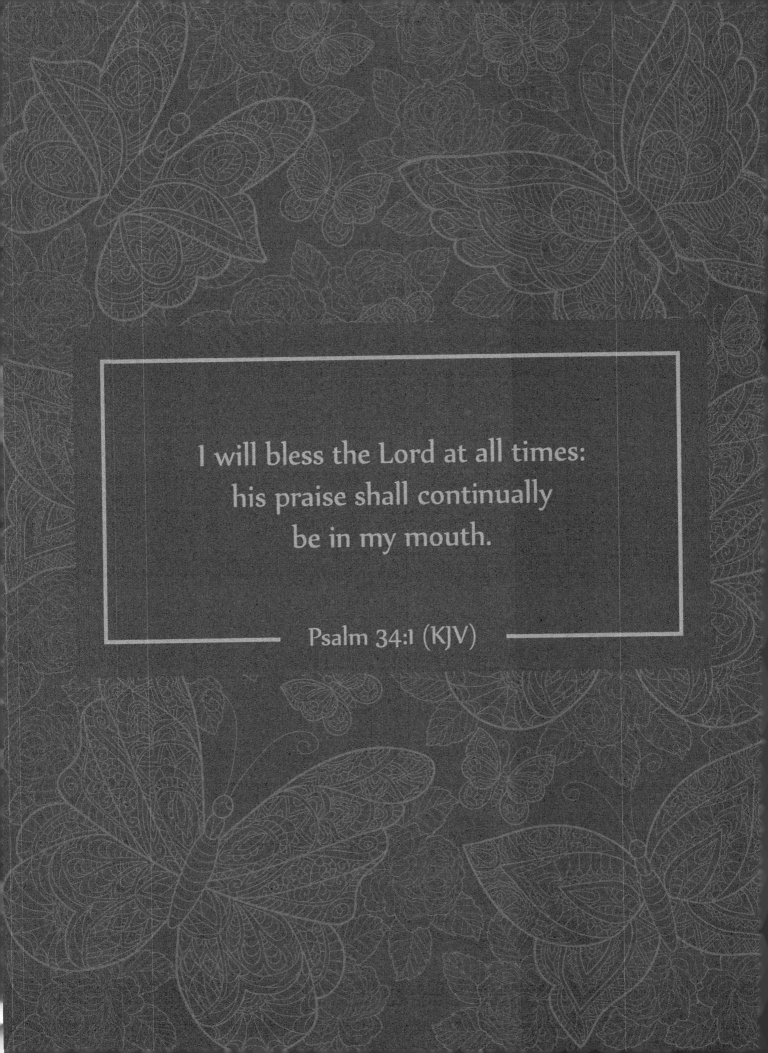

I will bless the Lord at all times:
his praise shall continually
be in my mouth.

Psalm 34:1 (KJV)

Deliver me from my enemies, my God;
protect me from those who rise up
against me. Deliver me from those who
practice sin, and save me from men
of bloodshed.

Psalm 59:1-2 (HCSB)

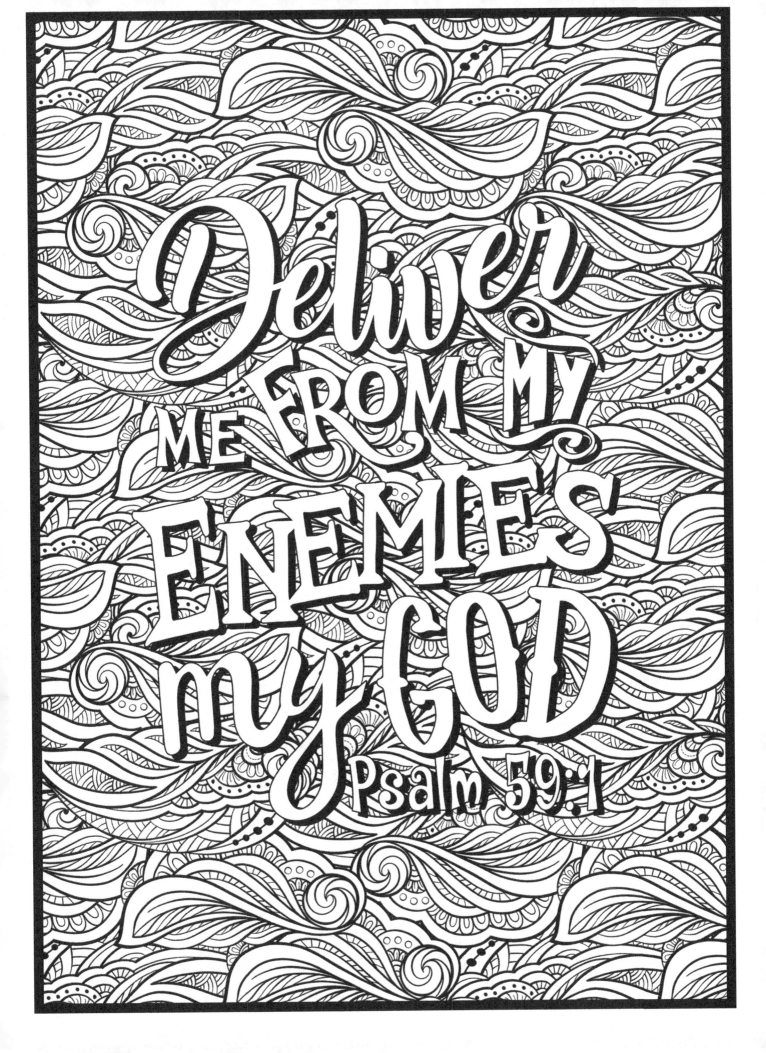

The words of the Lord are pure words,
like silver tried in a furnace of earth,
purified seven times. You shall keep
them, O Lord, you shall preserve them
from this generation forever.

Psalm 12:6-7 (NKJV)

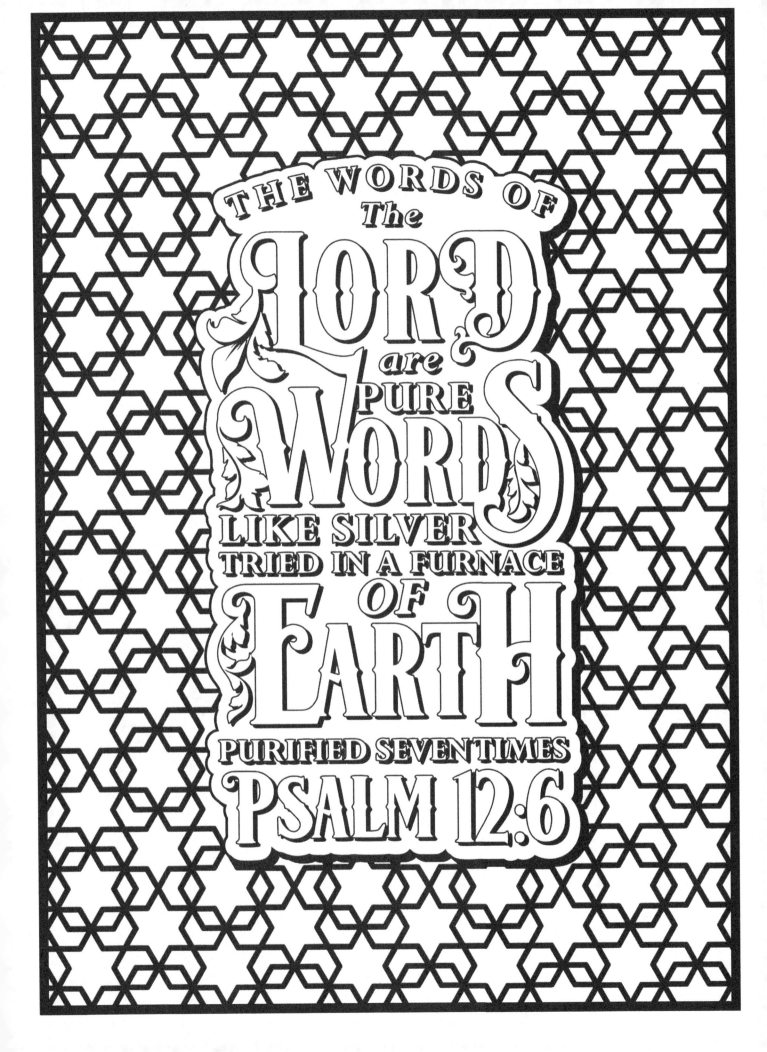

The earth and everything in it, the world
and its inhabitants, belong to the Lord;
for he laid its foundation on the seas
and established it on the rivers.

Psalm 24:1-2 (HCSB)

The Lord also will be a refuge for the oppressed, a refuge in times of trouble. And those who know your name will put their trust in you; for you, Lord, have not forsaken those who seek you.

Psalm 9:9-10 (NKJV)

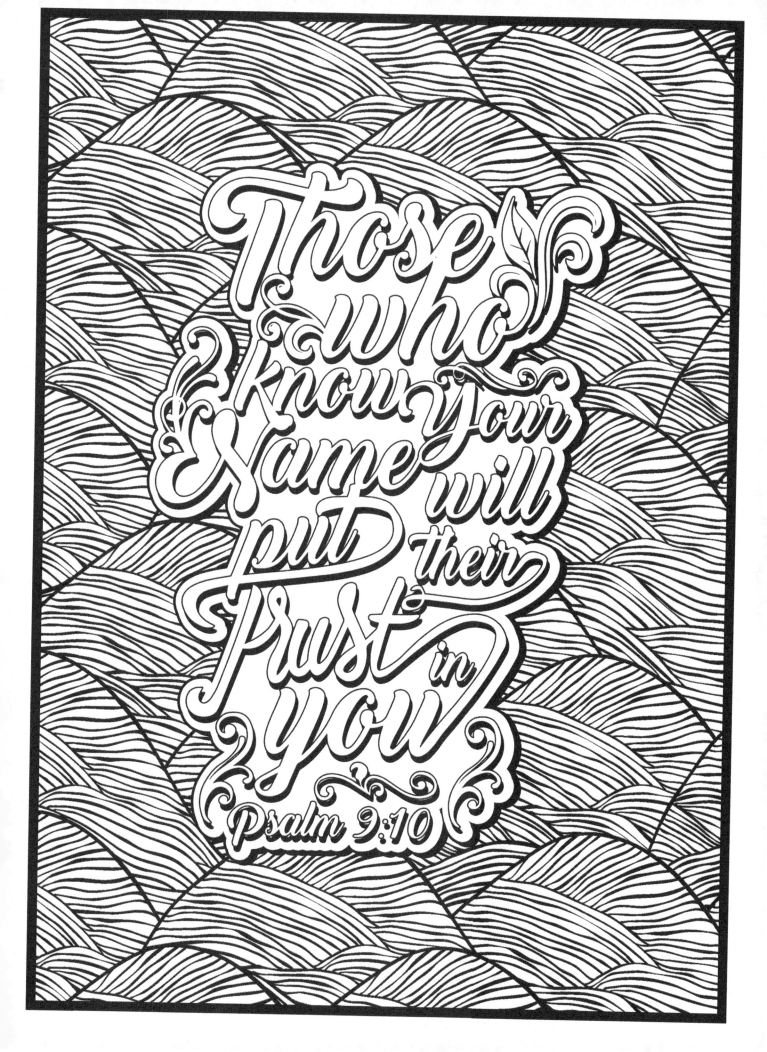

Those who know your Name will put their Trust in you

Psalm 9:10

You formed my inmost being;
you knit me in my mother's womb.
I praise you, because I am wonderfully
made; wonderful are your works!
My very self you know.

Psalm 139:13-14 (NABRE)

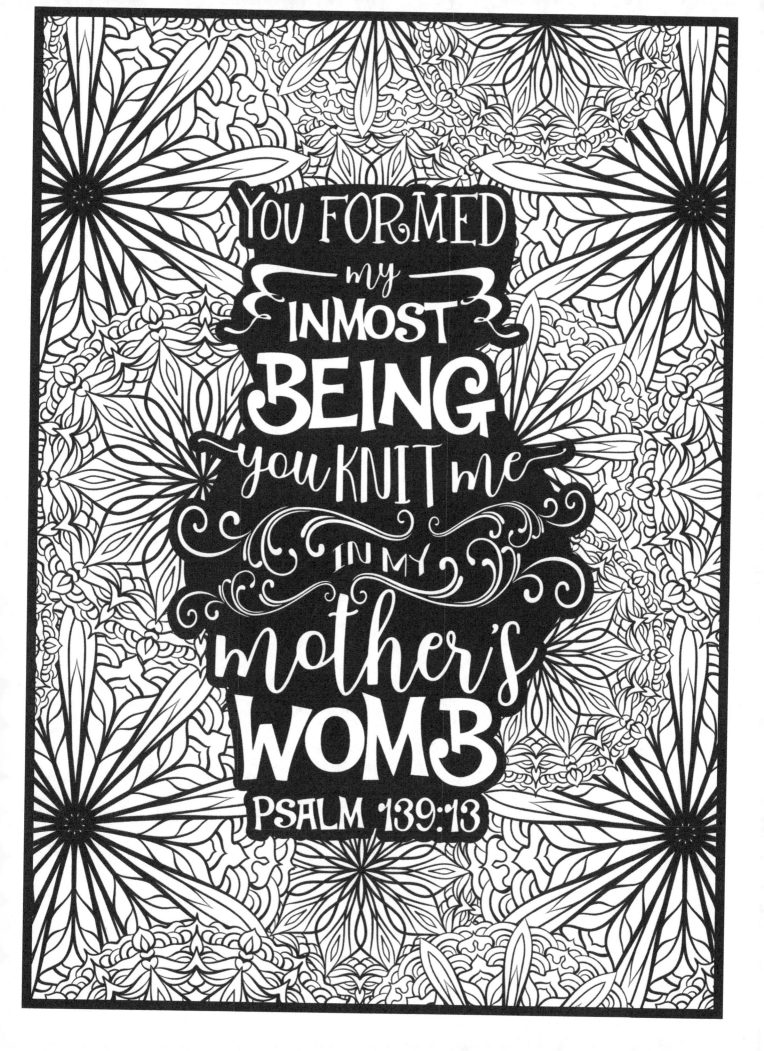

Thy Word is a lamp unto my feet,
and a light unto my path.

Psalm 119:105 (KJV)

You are not a god who delights in evil;
no wicked person finds refuge with
you; the arrogant cannot stand before
your eyes. You hate all who do evil;
you destroy those who speak falsely.
A bloody and fraudulent man
the Lord abhors.

Psalm 5:5-7 (NABRE)

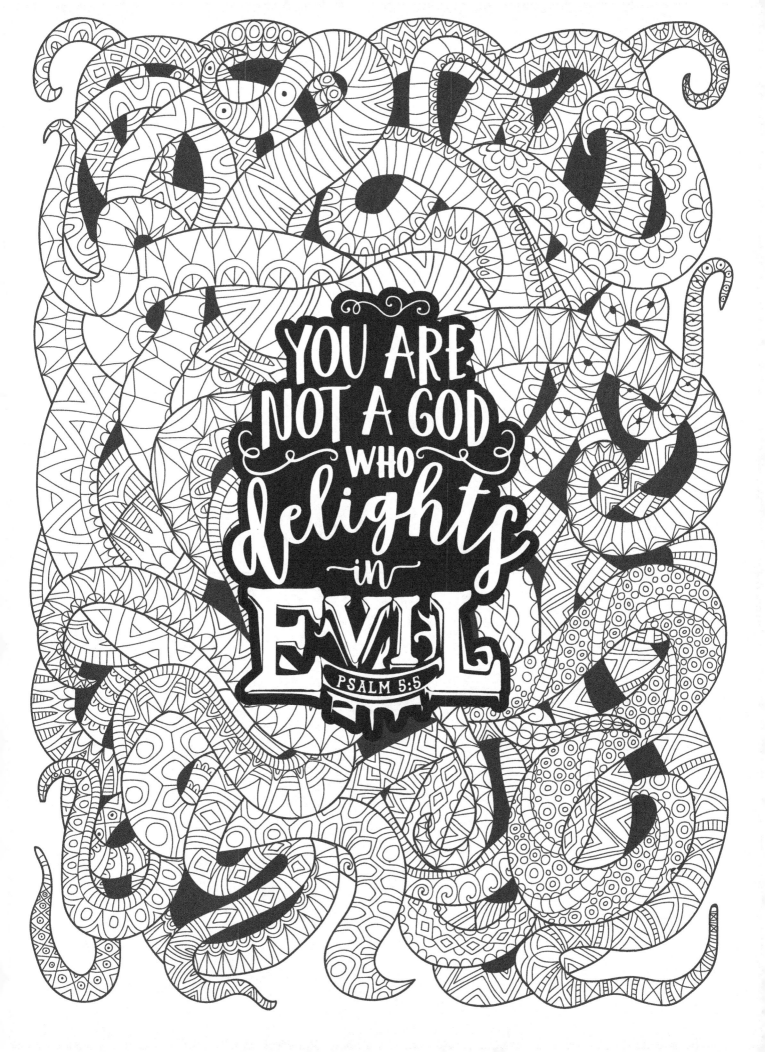

YOU ARE NOT A GOD WHO delights in EVIL

PSALM 5:5

As a deer longs for streams of water,
so I long for you, God. I thirst for
God, the living God. When can I come
and appear before God?

Psalm 42:1-2 (HCSB)

Shout with joy to the Lord, all the earth!
Worship the Lord with gladness.
Come before him, singing with joy.

Psalm 100:1-2 (NLT)

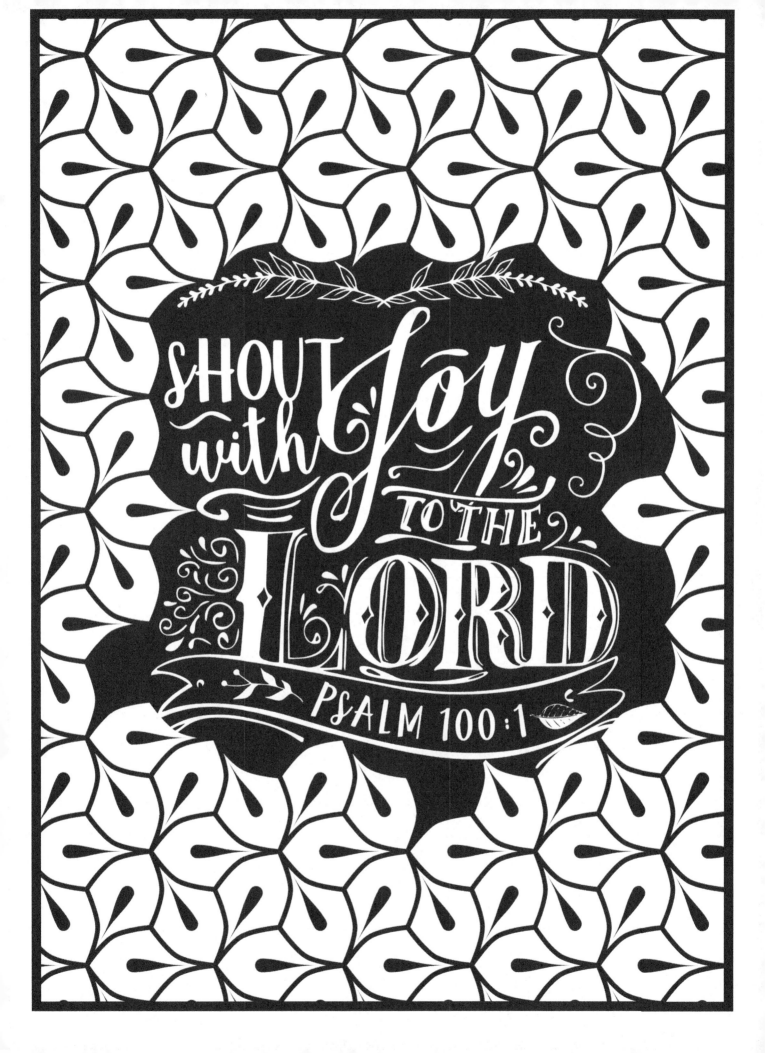

Even though I walk through the darkest valley, I fear no evil; for you are with me; your rod and your staff – they comfort me.

Psalm 23:4 (NRSV)

I call on you, my God, for you will answer me; turn your ear to me and hear my prayer. Show me the wonders of your great love, you who save by your right hand those who take refuge in you from their foes.

Psalm 17:6-7 (NIV)

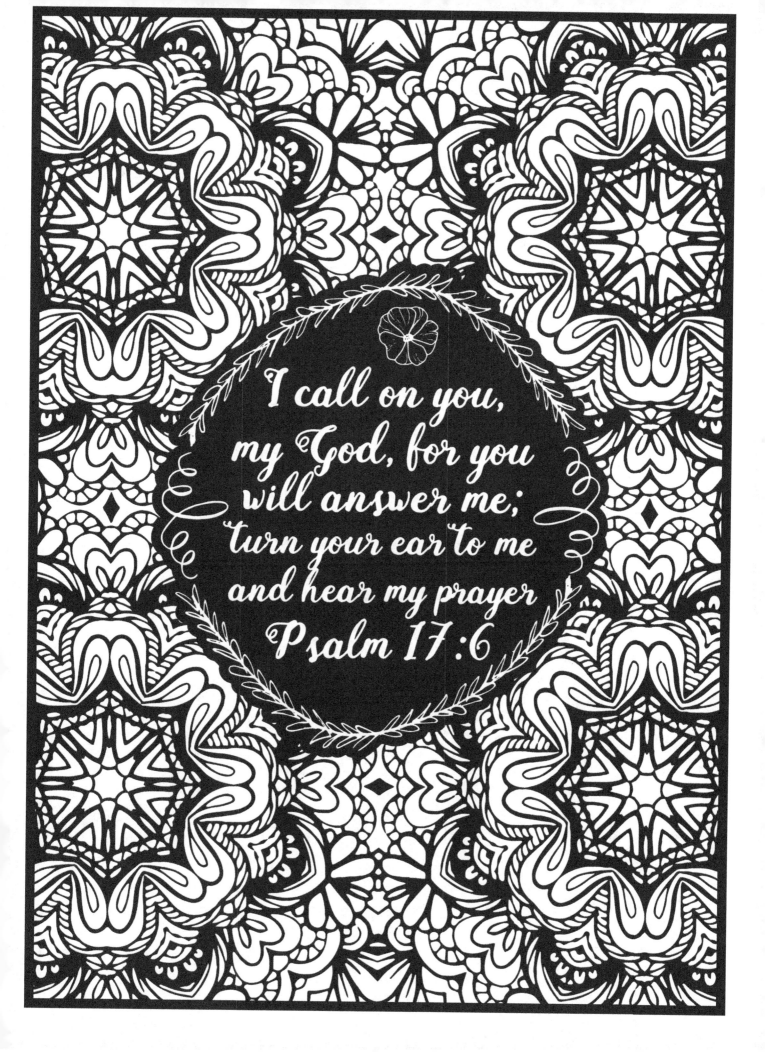

Let those who love the Lord hate evil,
for he guards the lives of his faithful
ones and delivers them from the hand
of the wicked.

Psalm 97:10 (NIV)

Search me, O God, and know my
heart; test me and know my anxious
thoughts. Point out anything in me that
offends you, and lead me along the path
of everlasting life.

Psalm 139:23-24 (NLT)

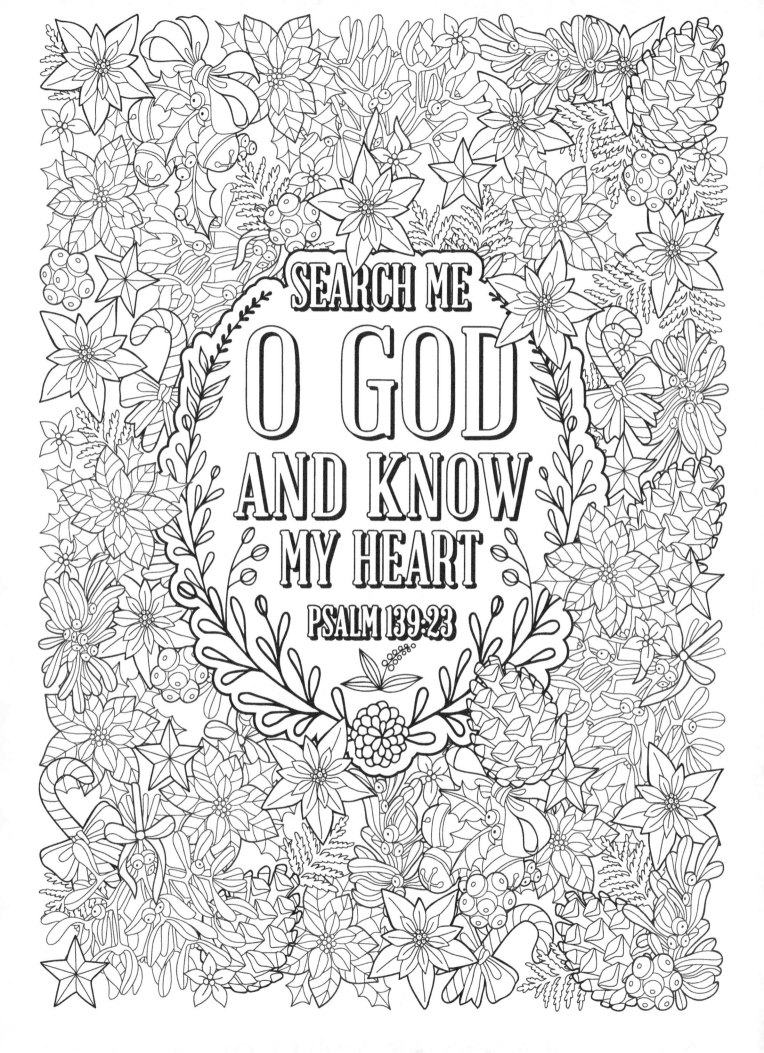

If you make the Lord your refuge, if you make the Most High your shelter, no evil will conquer you; no plague will come near your home. For he will order his angels to protect you wherever you go. They will hold you up with their hands so you won't even hurt your foot on a stone.

Psalm 91:9-12 (NLT)

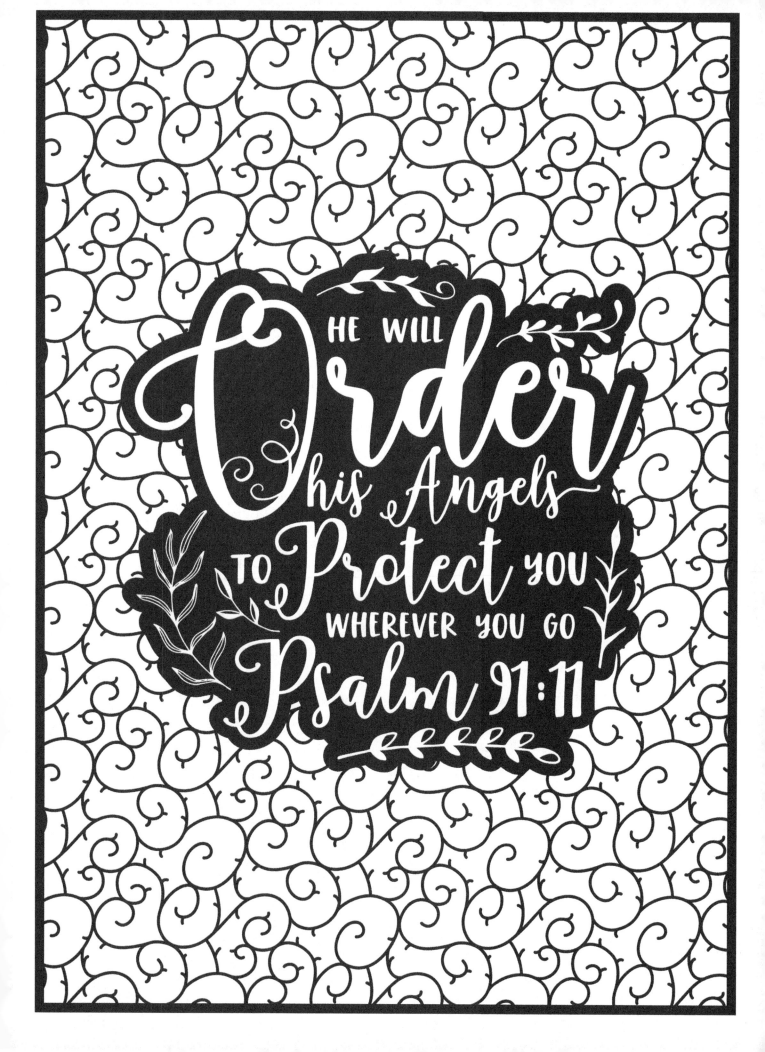

HE WILL Order his Angels TO Protect you WHEREVER YOU GO Psalm 91:11

The stone which the builders rejected has become the chief cornerstone. This was the Lord's doing; it is marvelous in our eyes. This is the day the Lord has made; we will rejoice and be glad in it.

Psalm 118:22-24 (NKJV)

I can never escape from your Spirit!
I can never get away from your presence!
If I go up to heaven, you are there;
if I go down to the grave, you are there.

Psalm 139:7-8 (NLT)

The law of the Lord is perfect,
refreshing the soul. The decree of the
Lord is trustworthy, giving wisdom
to the simple.

Psalm 19:8 (NABRE)

the law of
THE LORD IS PERFECT
refreshing
THE SOUL
PSALM 19:8

Be still, and know that I am God;
I will be exalted among the nations,
I will be exalted in the earth!

Psalm 46:10 (NKJV)

be still KNOW AND THAT I AM God

PSALM 46:10

The Lord is my light and my salvation –
so why should I be afraid? The Lord
is my fortress, protecting me from
danger, so why should I tremble?

— Psalm 27:1 (NLT) —

The
LORD is my LIGHT
AND MY SALVATION
Psalm 27:1

Happy are those who do not follow
the advice of the wicked, or take the
path that sinners tread, or sit in the seat
of scoffers; but their delight is in the law
of the Lord, and on his law they meditate
day and night.

Psalm 1:1-2 (NRSV)

Make your ways known to me, Lord;
teach me your paths. Guide me in your
truth and teach me, for you are the God
of my salvation; I wait for you all day long.

Psalm 25:4-5 (HCSB)

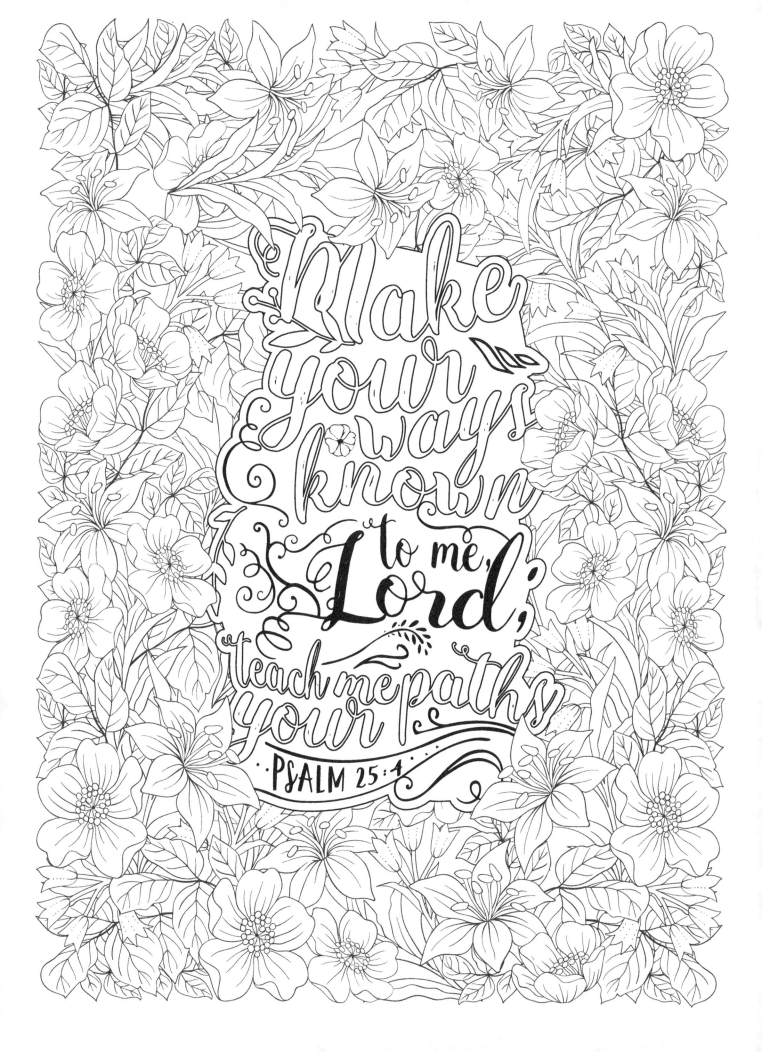

Make your ways known to me, Lord; teach me your paths

PSALM 25:4

The heavens declare the glory of God;
the skies proclaim the work of his hands.
Day after day they pour forth speech;
night after night they reveal knowledge.
They have no speech, they use no words;
no sound is heard from them. Yet their
voice goes out into all the earth, their
words to the ends of the world.

Psalm 19:1-4 (NIV)

Taste and see that the Lord is good;
blessed is the one who takes refuge
in him.

Psalm 34:8 (NIV)

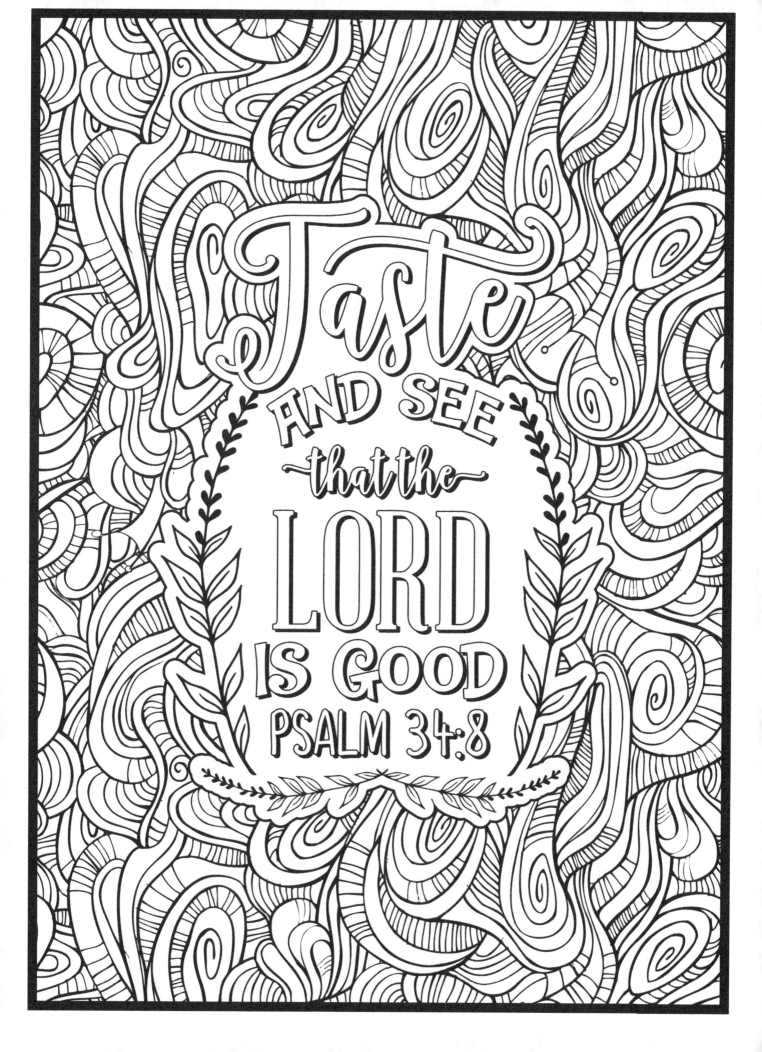

Why do the nations conspire and
the peoples plot in vain? The kings
of the earth rise up and the rulers band
together against the Lord and against
his anointed, saying, "Let us break their
chains and throw off their shackles."

Psalm 2:1-3 (NIV)

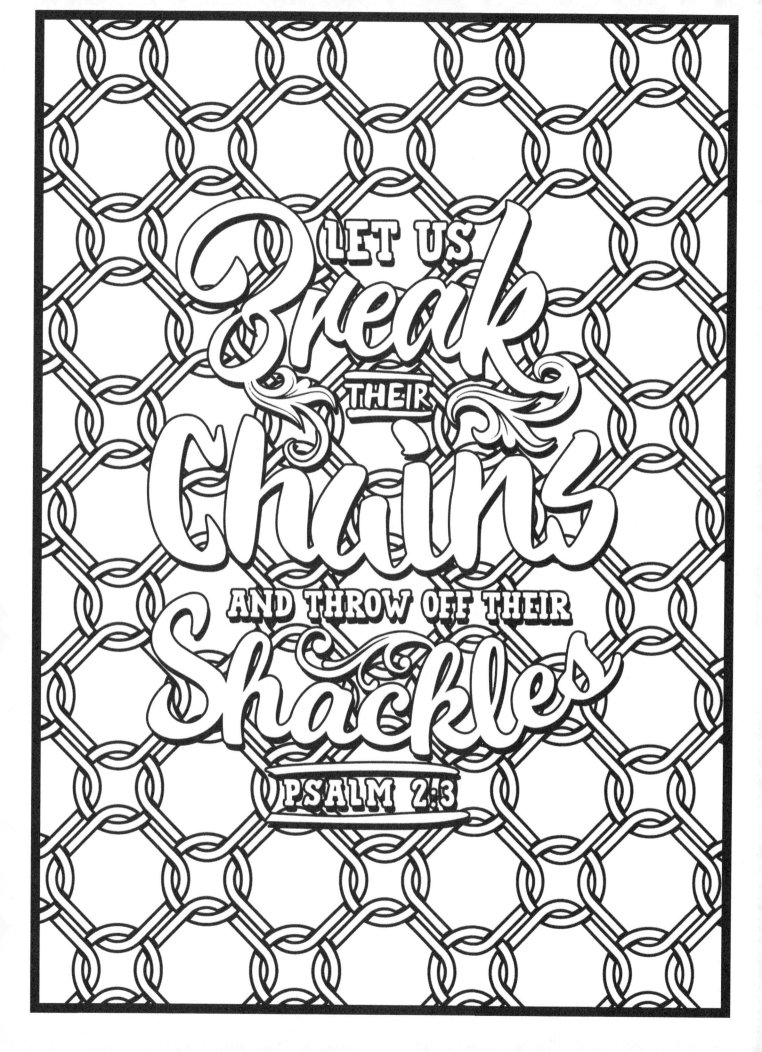

I lift my eyes toward the mountains.
Where will my help come from?
My help comes from the Lord,
the Maker of heaven and earth.

Psalm 121:1-2 (HCSB)

The fool says in his heart,
"There is no God."
They are corrupt, their deeds are vile;
there is no one who does good.

Psalm 14:1 (NIV)

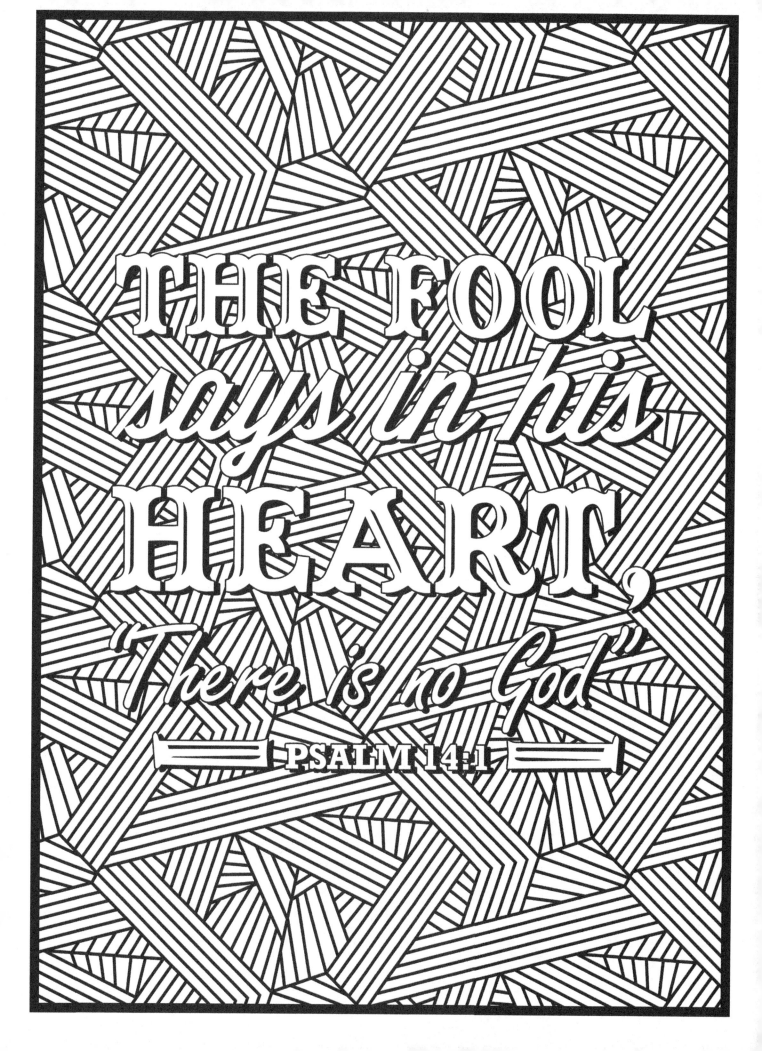

I remain confident of this: I will see the goodness of the Lord in the land of the living. Wait for the Lord; be strong and take heart and wait for the Lord.

Psalm 27:13-14 (NIV)

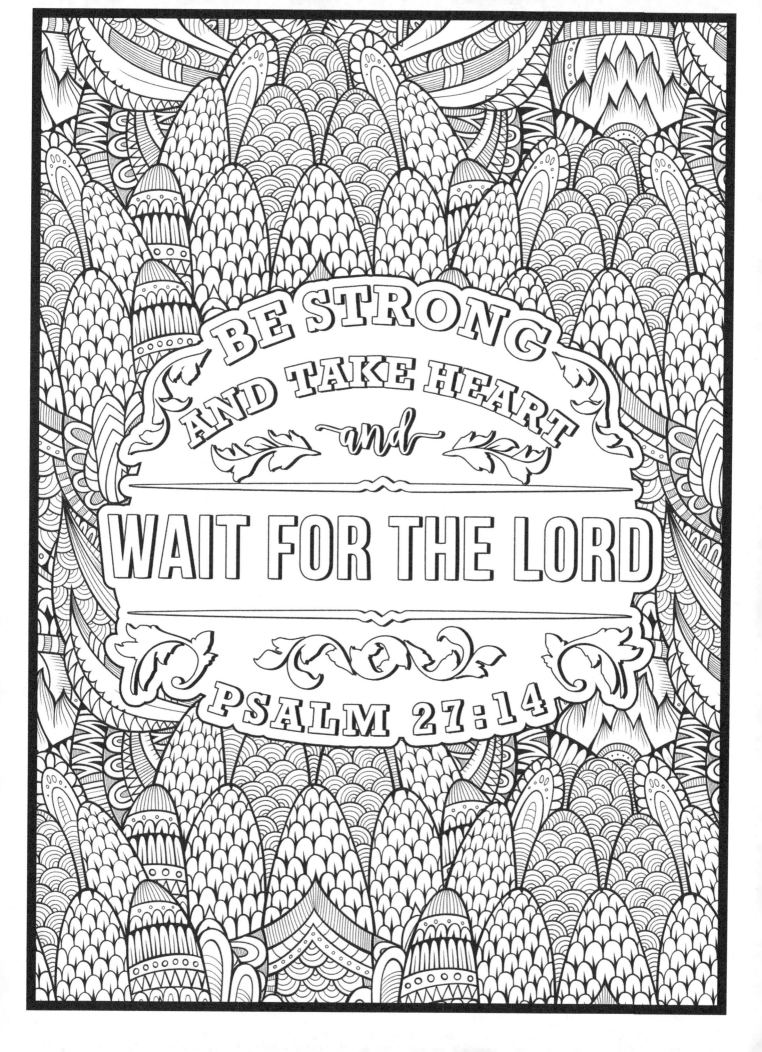

BE STRONG AND TAKE HEART *and* WAIT FOR THE LORD

PSALM 27:14

Free PDF
Download of this book

www.inspiredtograce.com/ctbpsalms

YOUR DOWNLOAD CODE: CTB9337

@inspiredtograce

Inspired to Grace

 Want free goodies?
Email us at freebies@inspiredtograce.com

 @inspiredtograce

 Inspired To Grace

Shop our other books at
www.inspiredtograce.com

Wholesale distribution through Ingram Content Group
www.ingramcontent.com/publishers/distribution/wholesale

For questions and customer service, email us at
support@inspiredtograce.com